Magic Places

pennie brownlee

the adults' guide
to young children's
creative art work

photographs
anne hocking
pennie brownlee

Published 1983 with financial assistance from the
International Year of the Child Telethon Trust.

Revised 1991
Revised 2004
Revised 2007. Reprinted 2009, 2010
Copyright © Pennie Brownlee 1983, 1991, 2007

National Library of New Zealand
Cataloguing-in-Publication data

Brownlee, Pennie, 1947 -
Magic places: the adults' guide to young children's creative art work/ Pennie Brownlee; photographs, Anne Hocking, Pennie Brownlee.
Rev. Auckland [NZ]: NZ Playcentre Federation, 2007.
    1 v.
    First ed. Published 1983
    ISBN 0-908609-57-4

Creative activities and seat work. I. Hocking, Anne. II. New Zealand Playcentre Federation. III. Title
649.51

Design and layout 2007 revision: Pennie Brownlee
Printed by Wyatt & Wilson Print, Christchurch

Playcentre
Whānau tupu ngātahi
Families growing together

Playcentre is a parent cooperative which offers quality early childhood education with opportunities for parents and children to grow and learn together.

Playcentre Publications
Producing books which support Playcentre Parent Education programmes - books for parents and for all early childhood educators.

Published in New Zealand by the
New Zealand Playcentre Federation
PO Box 15 886
WAITAKERE 0640
New Zealand

Phone/Fax 09 827 3469
E-mail publications@Playcentre.org.nz
Web: www.Playcentre.org.nz

*To Sue, Annie, Gail, Marylon,
Jill, Erica, Dawn, Lyn and June:
a fruit from our Summer at Playcentre.*

My thanks ...

to my Mum Peg who wouldn't let me trace, who gave me confidence in my creative ability, and who kept us supplied with plenty of paint and paper,

to my daughter Clare who started me thinking about children's art development,

to my great-nephew Keegan and great-niece Cameron for allowing me see the world afresh through their eyes,

to the children who allowed me to watch them and who let me have their work: Beau Barlow, Melanie Bell, Clare Brownlee, Garth Docherty, Paul and Justin Dufty, Keegan and Cameron Dufty, Angela and Mark Harris, Simon and Tim Jones, Jake and Jessie Henderson, Nancy and Virginia Loane, Kori Morehu, and Anna and Trudy Sharpe,

to Annie Hocking for her beautiful photographs,

to the big people and little people at Aniwaniwa who allowed me to photograph them and their Centre,

to Jo Kelly, Deidre Dale and Naomi Morton for their encouragement in getting the first edition to print,

and to the women at Thames-Parawai Playcentre. I learned so much as we talked, listened, laughed and worked our way through our season in Playcentre.

Foreword

This is a book about love and respect. It is about loving enough to set up the environment for our children which respects them as the miracles that they are.

When we who are guardians to the children love in this way, we allow the wellspring of creativity to flow in each of our children - and what we discover is that every child is an artist, every child is creative, and every child is - from within - a miracle.

We may even go so far as to work out that buried under all the layers of years and restrictions, we too are wellsprings of imagination, of creativity, of fun, and dare I say it, that we too are miracles.

The only future worth dreaming depends on our ability to learn to love and respect well enough, fast enough. This book offers one place to begin: loving and respecting the Creator in each Child, and in each one of us.

Pennie Brownlee
September 1989

Table of contents

My thanks — 3
Foreword — 4
Artist and miracle — 7

Part one

Four aspects of creativity — **8**
Experience and awareness — 8
Experience — **9**
Experience soaks in through the senses — 10
Creative thought unfolding — 11
Developing awareness through empathy — 12
Growing understanding and love — 13
Growing curiosity — 14
Rich experience, rich words — 15
Playful experience — 15
Focus — **16**
The ridiculous cat — 16
The unique cat — 17
In focus — 19
The creative process — **20**
Rules for adults — 20
The art product — **22**
Respect — 22
Writing on children's work — 22
Displaying children's art work — 23
Display basics — 23
Talking with children about their work — 24

Part two

Developmental stages of children's art work — **27**
Scribbling stage 0 - 6 years — **27**
Drawing, not scribbling — 28
Symbol stage 4 - 10 years — **29**
Problem solving — 31
Realism stage 10 - 11 years upwards — **34**
So-called creative activities — 35
Is it creative? — 38

Part three

Setting up a successful creative programme — **39**
Clay — 41
Playdough — 42
Painting — 43
Finger painting — 45
Collage — 48
Drawing — 50
Love, care and attention — 51
The bigger picture — 52
Magic places — 55
References — 56
More reading — 57

Every child is an artist. The problem is, how to remain an artist once he grows up.

Pablo Picasso

Artist and miracle

Every child arrives onto this planet both an artist and a miracle - every child - your child included. One way of appreciating just how miraculous a newborn child is, is to stop and ponder on brain cells. Each child is born with as many brain cells, neurons, as there are stars in the Milky Way galaxy. While some of these cells are already 'wired up' at the time of birth, by far the most of these cells are ready and waiting to be wired up **after** the birth. The more wiring up that happens - that is the more connections that are made between neurons - the greater the realisation of your child's potential.

That is where we adults come into it. We are the ones who oversee the **environment** that the child comes into, and we set up the **patterns of relationship** with our children - which either encourage them to meet their potential, or not.

To develop and grow as they are designed, all children have three great needs. They need **audio-visual communication**. That means from day one they need eye contact with us and they need us to speak gently with them. Allied to that, they need **nurturing**, which is another way of saying that they need tenderness and care, love and respect. Lastly, they need to **play**. Play is not an optional extra. Play is the activity that wires in all of the intelligences, and creative play is the highest form of play.

When we provide these, we are tending the seedbed of their creativity, watering the potential and making sure that their creative play is neither stunted nor trampled. We are fostering our children's natural development as Creative Beings.

Part one

Four aspects of creativity

experience
focus
the creative process
the art product

Creativity can be divided into these four aspects. We will look at each aspect separately so that we can understand both what we can do to **assist and support** creative development in our children, and what **children must do** so that they develop their creativity.

Experience and awareness

Every child is, at core, pure awareness. In their awareness they are like little sponges. They soak in all that is going on around them, with all of their senses. No one teaches them how to do this; it is part of being human. What they soak in will be the raw material from which they will draw when they are creating.

Playing on machinery in a hire-yard is a rich, exciting experience. Later, if Keegan wants to play at being a roading contractor, or if he wants to draw a roller or make a model of one, he will have a lot to call on because of all that he soaked in during his first-hand experience.

Experience

Having rich experiences makes us rich. It wires up those precious brain cells. A rich experience is one that uses all of your senses; it is the **real** thing.

Keegan could have read a book about a digger, or he could have watched a video, or even played a computer game. Fortunately for him, he was much luckier than that. He was taken to experience a **real** digger. He has soaked in all of the smells, the textures, colours, shapes, sounds - and much more. He knows in his body how it feels to climb in and to sit in the driver's seat. He knows how it feels to 'drive' it, moving the levers. He knows the sounds of the engine and the gears as it works.

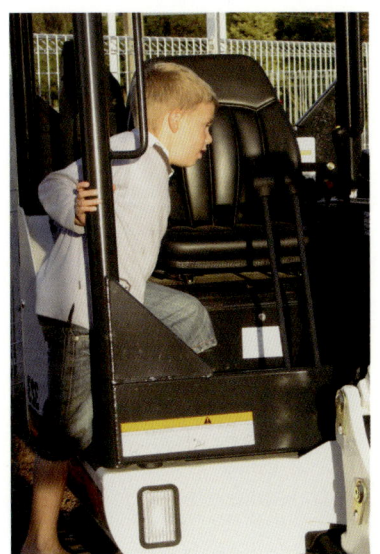

Later, in his imagination, he will be able to recall all of those rich sensory details, including the emotions he experienced when he was exploring the digger.

Experience soaks in through the senses

Consider this list of flower experiences. Have you ever …

>gathered wild flowers
>picked garden flowers
>sucked nectar out of blossoms
>pulled petals off flowers
>picked a flower to bits to see how it was made
>grown flowers from seed
>made an arrangement or a posy
>given flowers to say that you cared
>pressed flowers
>made a daisy chain
>smelled freesias, roses, jasmine, violets
>carried or worn flowers for a special occasion?

You probably answered *"yes"* more often than *"no"* indicating your wide experience with flowers. It is this experience, soaked in through your senses and now 'wired' into your brain, that will be the basis of your creativity.

> Television, videos and computers are not rich sensory experiences. They cannot provide what the young child needs to develop. At the very best, they are down-time for your child. Grow your child's potential by offering rich, **real** experiences.

Creative thought unfolding

Out of this experience we can begin to ponder and wonder. We can grow in our awareness and in our creative thinking. Have you ever wondered ...

>how a flower makes its colour
>how a flower folds into a tiny bud
>how it can unfold out of that bud
>how it knows how to make alive seeds
>how it makes perfume
>how it knows how to attract bees
>why some flowers last only one day
>why some flowers last weeks
>how come some flowers are minuscule
>how come some flowers are huge
>whether the flower is alive and can think
>how the flower plant knows how to make
>the same pattern flower - every time?

Children are natural 'wonderers' and natural scientists, and when we wonder alongside our children we stay tuned into the mystery of the experience.

When we are wondering, the answers are not important. It is the right question that matters. The right question doesn't have a right answer. The right question will generate awe and more wondering - exactly the state of mind of the scientist and the creator.

Developing awareness through empathy

We can also use awareness to ponder on what it might feel like to experience life from a different point of view. Have you ever thought about how it might feel for a flower to ...

> have a bee take nectar from it
> have a bee's feet crawl right down its throat
> be rained on
> be out in a hail storm
> close up at night
> open again when the sun comes out
> be picked off the plant
> run out of water in a vase
> have a nose come and sniff in its face?

All of this, and more, is there for our children from rich, real experiences. These experiences need not cost anything. The best ones are free from the natural world. Young children need countless opportunities to explore Mother Earth and Her treasures, growing their sense of belonging as a citizen on this amazing planet.

Our children are dependent on us for access to experiences. It is our job to see that they have rich experiences, and to provide more 'helpings' of experiences they have enjoyed. Conservationists are not born from one bush walk. A love affair with the bush, like any deep love, takes time to grow and develop.

Growing understanding and love

We can't know what our children will grow up to love, but we can be very sure that unless they have experience of something, there is no chance they could ever understand it or love it.

When Leela **plays** with a pine cone ...

>she soaks in the complex patterns of its structure
>she feels it with her hands and her skin
>she smells it and tastes it
>she feels it with her face, her mouth, her tongue
>she weighs it and gets a sense of its mass and its balance
>as she touches it she hears the different sounds it makes
>she watches the path it takes when it rolls
>she hears the sounds it makes when it rolls away from her.

She is filing all of this experience into her memory, making neural connections. When the next pine cone she picks up isn't as open as the previous one, she soaks in the similarities and the differences.

If Leela has many experiences with pine cones during her childhood, if she gets to ponder and wonder about the miracle of a pine cone, there's a very high chance she will get to understand and appreciate it.

Growing curiosity

Curiosity is a gift children come with. It's as if they know that they have trillions of brain cells to be wired up, and the best way to do that is to find things to **do**. The more things the better. To learn, children have to be curious - about everything.

The way we adults speak and behave can grow a child's curiosity and wonder, or it can kill it. Take snails for example:

> *They're just snails.*
> *Yuk. Slime. Get them out of here at once.*
> *We'll poison them.*
> *Argh! Squash them. Now.*

The toddler who was fascinated at how the snail moved, amazed by the iridescent trail, intrigued with the retractable 'horn eyes', in awe of how it could all fit back in its shell-house, now ends his love affair with the part of Life called snail.

Snails are neither good nor bad, snails are simply snails, and our role as wondering adults is not to judge, but to **just notice**. Our intuition is the most reliable guide to when to stay silent just noticing, and when to speak and wonder out loud. When we stay silent, children tune in their awareness and soak in the experience. When we wonder out loud, children grow their thinking and their vocabulary, so that they in turn can give voice to their wonder.

Rich experiences, rich words
As Keegan acquires language, he needs words to describe the things he has noticed about snails. He needs words which match the richness of his experience.

Our role is to use the richest language that we are capable of because children not only soak in their experiences, they soak in their vocabulary too. It is absolutely effortless for a young child to soak in an extensive, rich, working vocabulary - **if** that is what they hear.

Playful experience
When children live in the moment, experiencing the world around them with all of their senses, they are playing - that essential human activity which develops their intelligences and their spirit.

We too can learn from children by entering this state where we are totally engrossed in the moment-to-moment wonder of our world. This is the most natural learning state available to all of us.

As a bonus, these play-full experiences will be the basis of our children's creativity.

Focus

Having had rich experiences, the 'data' is in. All of the sensory data, vocabulary, emotions, precepts and concepts gathered during the experience are filed in the child's memory banks. Focusing is the act of 'opening the files' again, of **reliving the experience** so that all the details are available, ready to create from.

Remember at school after the summer holidays when the teacher said, *"Write a story about the holidays"* and your mind went blank? Of course you had plenty of holiday experiences to write about, but the blank just meant that the files were still closed. The teacher didn't get you to focus on your experience first: to talk about it, to recall and to relive it so that all the data was available to create from.

Sometimes children have those blanks, and when they do, they say, *"Do it for me"* or *"I can't do this."* This is when they need us to help them focus, to help them open the files.

The ridiculous cat

Imagine that a three-year-old asked you to draw a cat for her. You could comply and draw a cat for her, and it would probably look like this.

The three-year-old has plenty of experience of cats. She knows about cats and she has built up her own concepts of cats. By drawing for her you have taken away her opportunity to show you just what sort of cat she had in mind. You have taken away her chance to sort out her ideas about cats and how to get them down in symbol form. Worse, she may think that that is the only way to draw cats and model all hers on that particular one.

This applies not only to drawing, but to all creative activities including blocks, construction sets, clay, playdough, collage, carpentry, sewing .... If you do it for them you stop them learning and growing, and they won't think of themselves as someone who can give anything a go.

The unique cat

When a child asks you to draw for her, you will firstly have to show her that you believe she can draw it for herself.

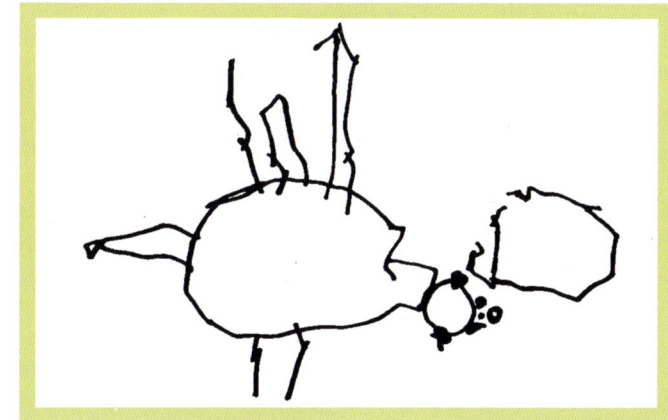

Clare:	*Mum will you draw Maui?*	
Mother:	*I'd rather see the cat you drew*	It is important that children see you value their art.
Clare:	*I can't draw it*	
Mother:	*Sure you can*	Let the child know that you believe she can do it.
	Where's a good place to start?	This question is the beginning of focus. Clare now has to sort around in her head and think about cats as she understands them.
Clare:	(Blank look)	
Mother:	*Fat tummy?*..	If you have to give the first suggestion, think of the most likely starting place, or the most likely suggestion to enable them to recall their experience. Always phrase it as a question that can be refused.

That was all the support that was given.

Clare began her drawing as her mother watched. Already, with just the body and the head drawn, it was obvious that Clare's cat was different from that which her mother would have done.

There followed a long silence as Clare thought about the next part. After she drew in the ears, there was an extremely long wait before the next addition. At no time did Clare look for help - clearly she was focusing her mind.

Well, she knew that her cat did not wear his features on the back of his head, but where to put them? Now it was obvious that Clare was visualising her cat from above. This bird's-eye view of things is common with young artists.

Two legs quickly followed - and her mother thought that she could count.

Then three more legs. Clare knows that cats have 'legs on each side'. Is that what leads to this viewpoint? The legs were followed quickly by the tail, and lastly a saucer of milk.

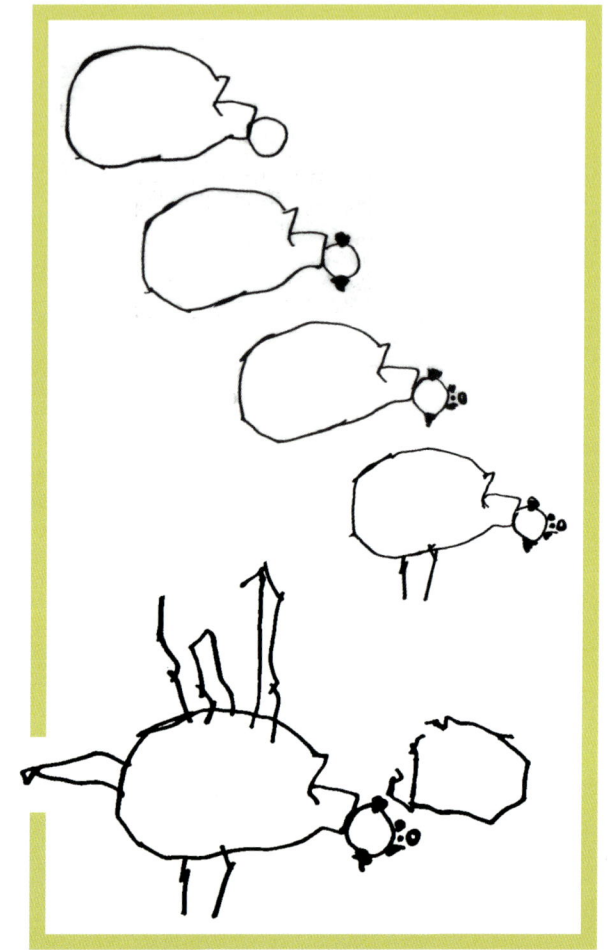

Obviously children are not going to want to draw something they know nothing about. If they want to draw something, or want something drawn for them, you can safely assume they have some experience and have a 'file' of the desired subject matter. They just haven't opened it yet. Like Clare's mother, you can help them focus so that they can get started.

What you definitely will **not** say is, *"What does it look like?"* or, *"Shall we find a picture to see what it looks like?"* These two responses are from your adult stage of development and they are totally inappropriate in the child's world view. Children are not focused on shapes, proportion, lines or perspective: their focus is the experience.

In focus

In a very relaxed way, get them talking and thinking about it, **get them reliving their experience**. That will be enough to help them move into the creative process - and what reward. Look at these magnificent cats.

The creative process

This is the climax of creativity. It is the special process where the work is done. The experience is reflected upon and new meanings are made. The medium is tried and tested, stretched and enjoyed, and the creation is a gift into this world. This is as true for our children as it is for Bic Runga, Janet Frame or Pablo Picasso.

> **The creating must belong to the child**
> No exceptions. It is in the creating that the value lies for the child. It is **their** process: they are reflecting on **their** experience, and they are making **their** unique expression into the world.

Any time an adult draws or makes for a child, they rob the child of this creative process, and the results can be devastating.

- The child loses confidence in his or her ability to create.
- The child's art does not develop through lack of practice.
- The child prefers to stay with 'safe' activities which take over the creative process, either through lack of confidence in their ability, or to avoid clumsy adult responses to their work.

The overall result is that one of the highest areas of human development is stunted for life.

Creative development can be salvaged at any point in life with skilful support, but the sad fact is that for most of the population this never happens.

Rules for adults

In order to avoid taking creativity out of the child's hands there are five simple rules.

> 1. **The child is the creator**
> We never draw, make or model for the child.

We also have to be really careful when working alongside children with children's art materials for our own pleasure. If, for example, I made a dragon out of playdough, I could expect the children to say, "*Make me one*." What am I going to say then? Am I going to say, "*No I won't,*" or am I going to do it for them and rob them of their creating? This brings us to rule number two.

> 2. **Stay in the scribbling stage when working alongside children**

This means we can experiment, make patterns and generally enjoy the media, but we won't make **any** particular **thing** so that they won't ask us to do the same for them.

3. **Children choose from *their* experience**
   We never tell a child what to draw, make or model.

Let's say I asked you to draw an aardvark. Think about it. It is (probably) impossible to draw outside your experience yet how many times do we ask children to do just that? Children will draw what is important to them.

4. **The child does it their way**
   We never tell them how to draw, make or model.

We know that different adults treat the same subject matter differently but somehow we can't accept that children do likewise. Many adults can't resist making additions and alterations to children's work. Any adult addition is part of the adult's concept and has no place on a child's creation. Ever.

5. **The child's creative potential is protected**
   We avoid presenting activities which rob children of their creativity.

Such activities include colouring-in books, tracing, worksheets, templates and picture stencils. We will look at these in more detail soon.

The art product

When the child has finished creating, she is left with a work of art which we will call the art product. Even though the creating is the really important part of the process, how we respond to the art product can either encourage, or even kill creativity. As we noted in the beginning of this book, every child **is** an artist. The problem is, how to **remain** an artist.

Respect

Children want from adults both respect and an interest in their work. Unfortunately, many adult responses to children's creating convey neither of these. Consequently, children are often left with the feeling that their work is being judged, and against standards they can neither understand nor meet. There's the sense that their work doesn't measure up. Many children take this a step further, believing that **they** don't measure up, and that they are not artists. So what does it entail, this responding respectfully?

Writing on children's work

If you **have** to write on children's work so that art works can be matched up with artists, one way to show respect is to use your neatest printing. The same goes if children ask you to write a story about their work, you use the very neatest printing you can manage. If the story goes beyond a few words, suggest that you write it on the back, or on a separate piece of paper so that you don't spoil the look of their painting. Children are very quick to note your respect for their work, or lack of it.

Displaying children's art work

Another way to show respect is to display children's creative work. Remembering that the creation is theirs, it is courteous to ask if you can have the artwork so that you can display it. Displays can be anything from one picture on the bedroom wall to a full-scale exhibition, a scrap-book of paintings, or a special shelf to show off models and treasures.

Display basics

Start with tidy
   If the paper is tatty or the painting needs trimming, do it tidily. That makes an enormous difference; so does keeping children's display boards and shelves tidy.

Frame it
   Frames really enhance art work and the simplest frame is a larger piece of card placed behind the work.
   Choose papers or cards that complement the colours of the creations being displayed.

Cards for any occasion
   Children's art work makes beautiful cards. When you encourage young artists to make cards for special occasions you let them know that you value their creations.

Eye spy
   Children view their work at eye level, the same as we do. They need us to set up a display board and a shelf at **their** eye level so that they can view their own work.

Fresh interest
   Keep replacing displays with fresh pieces. It keeps interest high and stops the display turning into 'wallpaper'.

Flying from its nest to a card, trying out different colours on the way.

Talking with children about their work

There are ways of speaking with children about their work which keeps the artist-inside alive and well, and there are ways that don't. Let's look the ways that don't first.

Praise and over-praise
We want children to stay centred in themselves, enjoying their creative play and what comes from it. Praise can be addictive and children can start creating for approval instead of for satisfaction. We don't want them always looking to others for approval of what they have done. It leaves them too vulnerable if their sense of value and worth is dependent on what others think. What is important is the quality of their experience and what they themselves think about it, so we need to respond in ways which grow creative self-assurance.

We never say, *"What's that?"*
It puts the child on the spot. If the child is working in the scribbling stage, the drawing won't **be** anything at all. If the child has made a symbol, they could wonder why you can't see what it is. After all, it's not up to children to have to work out that their stage of art development is different from ours, and then make allowances for us.

We never guess what a creative work is
Because of the way in which children construct their creations, guessing almost always means your guess will be wrong. Children build up a 'vocabulary' of symbols, patterns and formulae, and they combine these with new symbols as needed.

Nancy's people, and to the right, her dear little flounder.

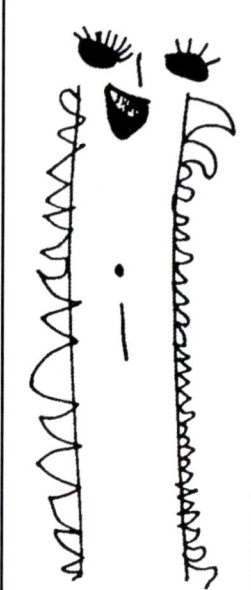

Jake and Jessie having a hug, and Jake's snapper

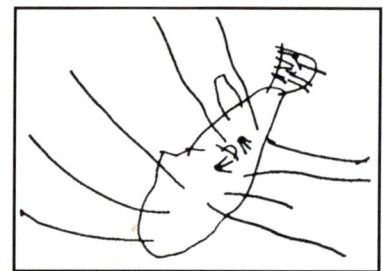

Observing Nancy as she explores a flounder, we get to see the connections she makes as she assimilates what she experiences. As young children often do, she gives a running commentary of what is going on for her. She notes that there are no feet, no eyelashes, no eyebrows and no nose. She examines the fins, tiny scales and its gills. Not ten minutes later she finds paper and sets out to draw the flounder.

We get to see her expressing this new experience, creating out of the repertoire she has developed. Using her basic person, she begins:

> ... his eyes ...   his eyelashes ...   his little nose ...
> ... his navel ...   his vagina ...   his legs ...
> ... and if I put these down his legs (fins),
> that will turn him into a dear little flounder.

Some of the things she consciously noted when looking at the flounder, like no eyelashes, were forgotten as she drew on her familiar symbol vocabulary.

Compare Jake's snapper with the drawing of him having a cuddle with his sister and you can see how he uses the symbol shapes he has developed. The important thing about the snapper for Jake was the needle sharp teeth. Put those in, add a few more 'arm and leg' symbols to stand for the spiny fins, and Jake's basic person becomes a snapper.

We never say, "*You don't draw cats like that.*"
Obviously the child does, and since each creation is a unique expression, you'd expect each to be different. If you were to view paintings of women by Frances Hodgkins, Edgar Degas or Mary Cassatt, you would probably like one better than the others. That doesn't make it better than the others though; it's different, and you like the difference.

This is the attitude to take and to model to our children so that they in turn will realise that their work is different from everyone else's. Not better, not worse, but uniquely different.

Different cats from different artists. None is better than another; each is different.

Now that we know what not to say, what can we say?
We can talk about the patterns, the texture, the shapes, the medium.
> *Looks like you had great fun going round and round and round with the pen.*
> *Look at that. That pattern you just made is called a chevron.*
> *Did you roll it to get that pattern in it?*
> *The clay is just right to poke your fingers in. Look at all those finger holes.*

If the child is still in the scribbling stage there is nothing else to talk about - but more about scribbling soon.

Things change when children reach the symbol stage. Rather than make subjective judgements about the children's work, get into the habit of commenting on what you observe, or what you **just notice**. More than anything else this keeps you present in the moment, and it conveys to the child that you are interested, you notice.
> So instead of saying, *"What a fantastic flounder,"* you might comment on the fins. *"I noticed that too Nancy, fins all the way around each side."*
> Instead of over-praising, *"Clever boy! What a marvellous bird,"* you might note,
> *"Lucky bird, you've given it really colourful wing feathers and tail feathers."*

If you suspect there is a story to the work and you want to know what it is, you can ask. But do it respectfully; phrase your query as a question which can be refused.
> *That looks interesting. Would you like to tell me about it?*

If I'm lucky they might want to tell me, but they might not. I don't always want to talk about my creative work either.

Just look
Sometimes I think we talk too much when children are trying to concentrate and create. If we let the child lead they will draw us in when they want to talk. Children sense our interest when we sit alongside them, stay present and just notice what they are doing. And when they have finished their creation, let them lead any talking. That way you'll grow a respectful partnership of equals; that's a very high form of creativity.

Part two

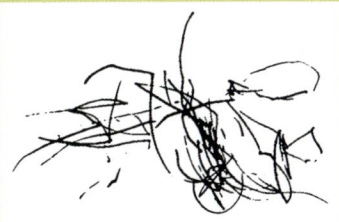

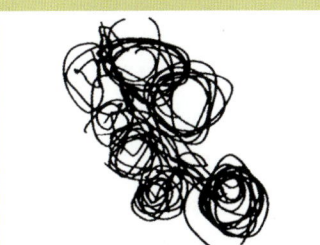

Developmental stages of children's art

Each child's development follows a universal pattern, and within that pattern each child's creations are unique. When we understand about the unfolding of this pattern (the stages), we are better able to support appropriately at each stage. The type of support required depends on knowing what to expect of a child working in a particular stage. The stages are developmental, so the chronological ages are **only** a guide; because not only are the creations unique to each artist, each artist follows his or her own timetable.

Scribbling stage 0 - 6 years

Every single artist in the world begins their artistic career as a scribbler. There is no other place to start. In this stage the child enjoys making marks, and has enough control to keep the marks on the paper. This is really a miracle when you think about it. The would-be-scribbler first has to discover they **have** hands, then they have to learn how to make their hands work so they can hold things like pens and crayons. Next, they have to learn how to let things go. Finally they learn how to hold the crayon, apply pressure and make marks.

And that is what they are doing - making marks. Children working in the scribbling stage are **not depicting anything**. Because they're not depicting anything, it is inappropriate to ask a scribbler, *"What are you drawing?"*
It is equally inappropriate to ask a scribbler to draw any particular thing: **they are making marks and patterns**. If you really want to appreciate what hard work this is, hold a pencil between your toes and try scribbling for five minutes without stopping. You'll have a new respect for the scribbling artist.

The word 'scribbling' doesn't have respect built into it though; it has negative connotations. Children soon understand that scribbling is a derogatory term and are keen to leave scribbling behind as soon as they can.

That is such a shame for the developing artist. Look at these six art works. Notice the control that is being developed as the artist explores shape and pattern. The motifs are being practised and combined. You can see the exploration of asymmetry and symmetry. The artist is building up a repertoire of basic shapes and patterns which will eventually be the foundation for drawing things, and for writing.

Drawing, not scribbling

So instead of using the word 'scribbling' with children, always refer to their work as drawing, pattern making, or design work. If there are older children speaking about younger children "*just scribbling,*" you can model to them: "*They are drawing. You used to draw just like that, and if they are ever going to get as good as you are, they'll have to do a lot more drawing like that, practising making patterns and shapes.*" That way there's a very good chance that children will keep exploring and creating patterns and designs for pleasure. We adults do that when we doodle.

We can encourage our budding graphic artists to stay in the 'design course', and play with design by making the most of everyday opportunities to decorate for decorating's sake:
>	carpentry models and clay models
>	balloons and sandcastles
>	cardboard boxes and box models
>	their own birthday cakes
>	drawing on steamed up windows or mirrors
>	envelopes to go in the mail ...

Symbol stage 4 - 10 years

Any time between the third or sixth year a new and magical development unfolds. Children suddenly realise that the lines and shapes that they create can actually **stand** for something. The lines and shapes are **not** Daddy, he is over there - but the lines and shapes **stand** for Daddy. They make a symbol. This is a huge conceptual shift. Now they will use all of the things they learnt as scribblers to make symbols to represent the things that are important to them.

Many adults now feel that real art development has begun and that they can help it along. What they do not understand is that the symbol stage is almost as far removed from the adult's own stage of development as the scribbling stage is. As we have already noted, children in the symbol stage are not concerned with the visual; they are **not** expressing what it looks like, they are drawing the experience that is important to them.

The shapes and lines are now combined to make symbols of people - and later of the things - that are **important to the artist**.

My bearded father.

My friend Jake and his little sister.

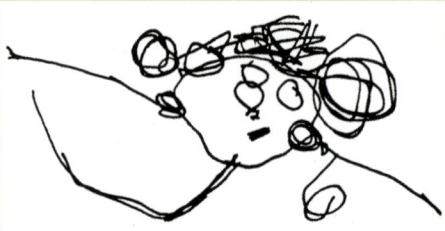

This artist was sick the night before and that is what she wanted to express. It was important to her - much more important than legs.

This artist knows about fingers, and although she knows about counting, it isn't important for this joyful creation.

It doesn't matter to a symbol maker that you can't see the baby inside a pregnant woman, or that you can't see through house walls to see the furniture. Like symbol makers from many different cultures, this artist uses x-ray pictures to express what she knows.

When **symbol makers draw what they know and what is important to them**, their pictures will not be in proportion, or the 'right' colours, or even logical to an adult way of thinking:
> *It doesn't look like that*
> *Her hands are too big*
> *Cows aren't that colour*

Comments like these show that the adult does not understand the symbol stage and is commenting from his or her stage of development, the realism stage. Such comments are not helpful to the child and can damage the child's confidence.

She knows there are four doors so she draws them.

Problem solving

Drawing what you know and what is important to you can pose problems. Watch these two young artists meeting problems and solving them.

When you are three-years-old, how do you draw a person waving?

Clare had been on a journey over the Tapu Hill, and so the hilly road is drawn first, then the car, and then the wheels. Clare has moved on from the stage where she drew all four doors on the car. She has developed her understanding and draws only the two doors which are visible from the side view of the car. She does not apply this new understanding to wheels yet.

On looking at her drawing she said,
    But it won't get up the hill.

She added more wheels which solved the problem of getting up the hill but presented another. A car with eight wheels? Pointing to the middle four wheels she said,
    This is a pram parked behind the car and you can't see it.
    Only the wheels.
Problem solved.

The mother and the father are getting married. They are so happy.

Before she had any pains.

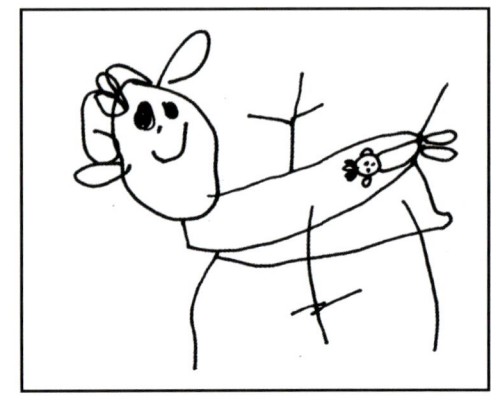

Angela did this series of drawings in approximately ten minutes. Some of the details that she usually drew on people were omitted, and you will note that some of the details like feet and hands are included out on some of the people some of the time. The omissions don't detract from the story or from the vitality of this five-year-old's comic strip. You can see that drawing babies in prams posed Angela a few problems which she solved in her own way.

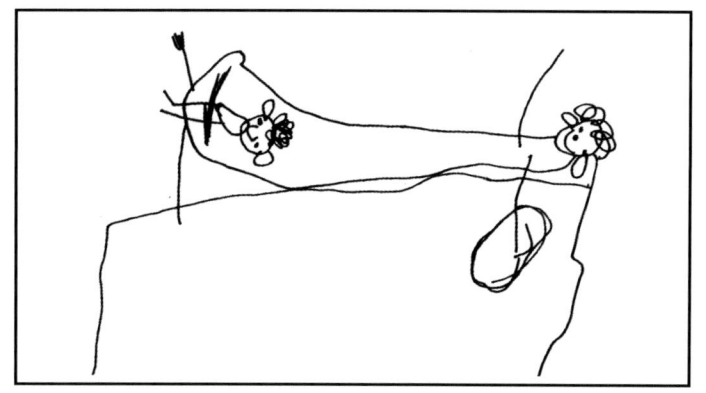

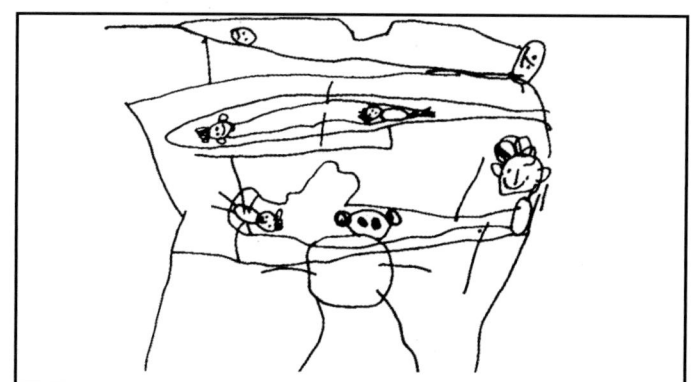

The father is so very happy.

The mother and the father are so happy with their new baby that they dance around the bedroom.

Realism stage 10 - 11 years upward

We adults are in the realism stage, and artists in the realism stage draw what they **see**. They want what they are drawing to be realistic, exactly the same in shape, perspective and colour as what they are looking at. It is important to the artist in this stage of development that what they draw **looks like** what they are drawing. The more that it looks like the subject, the more pleased the artist will be. And that is why, unless we know better, when our children have trouble getting started drawing we will ask, *"What does it **look** like?"*

Beginning realism

Young artists head slowly toward the realism stage as we have already seen with Clare. First she drew cars with four doors because that was what she **knew**, then later she drew them with two doors because that is what she **saw** when she was side-on to a car.

With experience, the things that children draw are placed within a context. They do this by drawing a ground-base line for everything to sit on, and a sky-ceiling line at the top of the picture. Later still, both of these lines are replaced with a horizon line.

For younger artists, things that are important are always big and central. As older children tackle perspective, things in the background are depicted smaller, even if they are important.

But by ten or eleven children have reached the stage in development where they, like you, want their work to look exactly like the subject.

No longer content to draw a symbol of dandelions like this, ▸ an artist in the realism stage wants the flowers to look real, to be recognisable as dandelions.

So-called creative activities

Anything which hinders or prevents children's progress through their developmental stages has no place in the home, early childhood centre, or school - not if we want our children to remain artists once they grow up.

There is a variety of creative and so-called creative activities available for our children, and adults need a way to judge which is which. Ask yourself:

Does the activity take the creative process away from the child?

If the answer to this question is yes, then the activity cannot be considered. Adults who do not understand how to keep creativity alive and well in children rationalise their presenting so-called creative activities.

So-called creative activities include colouring-in books, colouring-in worksheets, picture stencils, cut-out shapes for the children to colour in or stick things to, tracing, templates to draw around and then colour in.

It is helpful to look at these activities and some common arguments put forward in their favour, and then relate them to what we know about children's art.

Neither of these adult drawn fish pictures has the vitality of the bottom fish. It was drawn by a five-year-old.

Colouring-in books and colouring activity sheets
On the far left is a fish to colour in. Like the majority of these activities presented to children, the quality of the art work is poor and does not, indeed could not, take into account any child's experience of fish.

Colouring in teaches children to stay in the lines, it develops their muscle control
Children learn the skill of colouring in by colouring their own drawings when they are ready. When they **are** ready, they take far greater care colouring in their own creations. Notice the care that Keegan has taken colouring his fish at the bottom of this page.

Colouring in teaches children to use the correct colours
Children do not use the 'correct colours' until the 'correct colours' become important to them.

Colouring in keeps children quiet
True, colouring in does keep children quiet. So does cutting up the curtains, playing in makeup and picking off the wallpaper. Being kept quiet is not the criteria by which to judge the value of children's activities. When children do their own creating they are just as quiet, and there is value in the activity for them.

Shouldn't they be allowed to colour in for fun?
Of course they should. They should not only be allowed, they should be encouraged, and this is why it is so important that the scribbling/design/pattern making stage continues. Drawing and colouring their own patterns is creative, relaxing and fun. It is re-creation in the true sense of the word. Their pattern making flair is then incorporated into their symbols, as with this colourful fish on the left.

Colouring in doesn't hurt anyone
Most people, from about five years and older, are nowhere near their art development potential. Because of past damaging 'art' experiences, colouring in included, these people need specialist tuition to set them functioning again in the graphic arts. It's ridiculous to say that these activities don't hurt anyone. The only ones who are not damaged are those with above-average creative confidence and artistic ability. They manage to survive in spite of these activities.

Cut-out shapes for the children to fill in
It teaches them coordination
Cut-out shapes, like colouring in, is busy work for children. It keeps them quiet but does not offer them anything for their learning and development. If children have experience of fish, they can draw, cut out and decorate their own. It's hard to imagine why anyone would spend all that time and effort making things for children when children can do it better for themselves.

Tracing
Tracing is not common in younger children. The desire to trace comes about when older children want artistic success. Usually, the level of the child's own drawing is so low through lack of practice and encouragement that the child is embarrassed by his or her efforts. Encourage older children - eight years plus - to draw their own pictures:
> look at the overall shape, and lightly record that
> then work in the details.

The proportions in the finished drawing are usually so much better that the child regains confidence and tracing dies a natural death.

which way is up?

Templates

Templates can be very confusing for children and adults alike: which way is up? Here, the concept 'goldfish' is encased within an outline drawn by an adult, at the adult's stage of development, far removed from the child's understanding. It is not unusual for a child to pick up a template, turn it around and ask, *"What is it?"* The child has no idea what the template represents, yet with plenty of 'fish experience' all children will draw unique fish, the right way up, and they will know exactly what they are.

Is it creative?

If you can answer **yes** to these questions, the activity you have chosen is creative and will grow children's creativity.

- Are they doing this because they chose it, responding to the creative impulses arising from within their being?

- If they do this will it be their own, original in:
    concept and execution?
    shape and form?
    colour and decoration?

- If they do this will they be doing it their way?

- If they do this will they extend themselves?
    Will they learn more about themselves and their world?
    Will they learn more about the medium and technique?

Yes? Congratulations. You have chosen a creative activity.

Part three

Setting up a successful programme

Our children need us to set up the materials and maintain an environment which enables them to unfold their creativity. In most schools and early childhood centres adults set up the play areas in ways that **prevent** the children from fully developing their potential. Unfortunately, it is the rare exception to visit, or hear of, a play area in which the children could develop past a level of mediocrity, - though that is certainly not what adults intend.

It doesn't cost much in terms of dollars and cents to set up play areas of excellence. Indeed, it may even cost a lot less than is being spent at present. What **is** required is a basic knowledge of the various media, and lots of love, care and attention to both the media and the play environment.

Take clay for example. In many early childhood centres and most schools, clay comes out once in a blue moon. The following blue moon the clay reappears, and the child starts at the beginning again, developing clay skills. On the next blue moon, and by now it is quite possible that the child is in year seven at school, the child has to begin again because the opportunity to practise has been denied.

At four, Anna was an accomplished potter. She had opportunities that most children do not have. Her interest began when Anne Russell, herself a potter, undertook to care for the clay area. She bought **quality clay**, arranged suitable storage, maintained the clay at premium working consistency and kept the table orderly and inviting during session time.

At four Anna was an accomplished potter and sculptor. Notice the basic skills she has used to make these tiny figurines, the lidded treasure box and pinch-pot, and the miniature teaset on its separate tray. The teapot is the size of a tiny pea.

Anna so loved clay play that her mother bought clay for her to play, practise and create as much as she wanted to at home.

When Anna visited another centre she headed straight to her favourite, the clay table. She tried to work with the inferior clay and became frustrated to the point of tears because the clay would not do what she knew clay **should** do. The children at the host centre could not possibly develop their potential because the adults had, unwittingly, set it up so that they couldn't.

Get practical: love and care
Like Anna, children are honoured when adults love enough and care enough to pay attention, providing media and environments of excellence. Love, care and attention translate into practical details which are easily accomplished by each one of us. The following pages outline the requirements of a **basic creative programme**, which must be available for every child for the duration of every session.

Children, like Anna, use the basic programme to practise and build up their skills. Having developed their **basic skills** they can add to them, extend on them, and grow more skilful.

> The frills of creative play - for example novel techniques - are of very little use to children who have been denied the opportunity to develop their basic skills.

Clay

Many adults ask whether it is necessary to provide clay if they provide playdough. Playdough and clay do share some of the same qualities, but not many. Playdough doesn't do what clay does; it does not enable children to model and sculpt in the same way as clay does.

- A basic clay programme begins with **high quality clay**. Find a potter or clay retailer who will advise you which clay to purchase for small fingers and for low wrist strength.
- A **damp sponge** placed alongside each workplace provides enough water for young potters so that they don't drown the clay. The picture to the right shows a clay table all ready for the children.
- While a **whiteboard surface** is very suitable, canvas covered boards work well too. The clay does not stick to canvas so readily.
- Clay is a plastic art in which the artist uses fingers and hands to create. The basic programme begins with good clay - grey, white or red. Add water and the artist's hands. That's all.

The artist has to build up clay skills and learn the properties of clay. Children are a long time pushing and poking, squashing and messing, pressing and generally getting the feel of clay. They learn the skills of rolling ropes of clay, forming coils, making spheres, patting it smooth, making impressions, rolling the clay flat, pinching and 'milking'. When children make the transition from the exploring, experimenting stage to the symbol stage, they have all of these skills to call on to make clay models.

Honest talk
When the children make spheres and spirals, name them spheres and spirals; they are not 'marbles' and 'snails'. Using geometrical names enables children to become aware of the shapes in their world.

Basics, not frills
Children who attend centres where the clay table is covered with an assortment of tools such as knives, rollers, garlic crushers and forks, can graduate to school without ever having really touched the clay. You cannot build basic clay skills if you don't play with the clay with your hands.

Nor is the clay table a place to whack away with pounders to relieve frustration and aggression. That is about as appropriate as whacking your anger out on the piano with a hammer. The clay table is a place to relax and enjoy, to create and develop.

Keeping clay workable
With a little care, clay can be kept workable for at least a term. Store it in a plastic bag, covered with a damp cloth, inside a plastic bucket with a snap-on lid.

When the clay is beginning to get too stiff for little fingers, take a softball-sized piece, indent it with your knuckles, pour water into the hollows and then knead it back into the proper consistency.

Playdough

Playdough meets some of the children's modelling needs and many parents find playdough easier to provide at home than clay. Older children can help make this easy recipe.

Quality playdough

Mix together in a saucepan

- 1 cup flour
- half a cup salt
- 1 cup cold water
- 1 tablespoon cooking oil
- 2 teaspoons cream of tartar
- 2 teaspoons food colouring

Stir all ingredients over a medium-high heat until the mixture gathers together in a glob exactly as choux pastry does.

Knead immediately.

Store in an air-tight container. It will keep indefinitely.

Painting

Painting
Painting
Painting
Painting
Painting
Painting
Painting
Painting
Painting
Painting
Painting
Painting
Painting
Painting

Painting is a colour experience. It is about exploring in colour. The artist chooses the colour, applies it, then chooses another. The colours mix and change. This is the pure colour magic that is painting. To get the painting basics, children need good quality paint, and they need specific colours to play with so that they can experience colour alchemy.

Set the paint out in the order shown above. The artist has the primary colours - yellow, red, and blue - and they have the secondary colours - orange, purple and green. White and black allow children to experiment with tints and shades. The bottom picture shows the same set of paints, but they are set out in a different order so that is not easy to see or 'soak in' the relationship between the colours.

Painting basics

- The first consideration is where the easel is situated. Painters need to be **out of the traffic flow** so that they can concentrate without people running and pushing past them.
- Each painter needs to have a space at **their own easel,** and the easel will be white. When setting up colour experiences, always provide white surfaces to work on.
- Each painter will have the same **range of bright clean colours** to choose from, as is shown on the preceding page.
- The painter will **be able to *see* the colour** in the container, so that he or she can **choose** which colour to use. Those little paint pot lids, with holes in them so that the paint does not drip or spill, were not designed for artists. None of us would chance our luck buying an unmarked tin of paint if we were going to decorate. We would want to know exactly what colour we were buying.

- Because young children have to paint at an easel, the **paint will be creamy** in consistency so that it stays where they put it. It needs to be just deep enough to cover the bristles of the paint brush.
- The **brushes will be** the ones with the shortened handles, **tailored to suit children**.

Young artists in the scribbling stage need larger brushes because these artists want to get the most possible paint on in the shortest possible time. Artists in the advanced scribbling and symbol stages want finer brushes so that they can get the details, features and decoration to their satisfaction. It may be enough for older children to know where the smaller brushes are kept so they can help themselves when they want to paint finer lines.

Finger painting

Fingerpainting is a touching, feeling, colour experience. What children need to get fingerpaint basics is fingerpaint which feels good and looks good. The secret to getting it **feeling good** is in the making and the stirring.

- Into a large bowl put 2 cups of cornflour and 1 cup of cold water.
- Whisk it until all the cornflour is suspended.
- Boil the kettle.
- While stirring the cornflour and cold water mixture, add the boiling water very quickly, and stop when the mixture 'grabs'.
- Stir thoroughly until the mixture is smooth, thick and translucent.
- Gradually stir in up to a quarter of a cup of soap flakes, and mix thoroughly. The mixture will go white and thin down.
- If it is still too thick add a little water, stirring constantly until the fingerpaint is smooth and creamy. It will keep for up to a week in an airtight container in the fridge.

Divide the mixture evenly into three containers and add one heaped dessertspoon of tempera powder to each container and stir. The secret to getting it **looking good** is tempera powder. Tempera gives it the strong opaque colour which is ideal for experimenting with colour mixing, tints and shades. The tempera colours you need are a **cool red**, a **cool blue**, **lemon yellow** and **white**.

Food colouring makes a translucent mixture, and is okay for a change. It does offer novelty value because the fingerpaint looks and mixes differently.

- **Fingerpainting is a colour experience**, so children work on white surfaces; then they can see all the subtleties as the colours mix.
- **Children need their own white board** to work on if they are going to have the time and space to make their own discoveries, at their own pace, without interruption.
- Children enjoy **communal fingerpainting** every so often, where the paint is put on the table and everyone joins in. There is no chance of staying as long as they might like to, and no chance to work uninterrupted, but add music and this is great fun for a change.
- Fingerpainting is a chance to *experience* colour theory. No one has to teach children this - they learn which colours make which, soaking in how the colours mix and change as they play.

To facilitate this, give them any two of the primary colours and a pot of white. By way of a change, substitute the white with black and there is a whole new range of shades to discover.

Occasionally, put out three primary colours or three secondary colours. The paint will end up a mucky brown-grey. That too is an important learning, but you wouldn't want to learn it every session.

Children do not need to know any of these technical terms, but they **do need you to put out the right colours** so they can make these discoveries for themselves.

blue and red make purple
yellow and red make orange
yellow and blue make green

Fingerpainting is usually the artist's introduction to print making.
Heavy grade paper or card, placed on the finger painted pattern and pressed, results in a print of the painting. Very young children can have print making success this way.

It is not always necessary, and probably not desirable, to take prints every time children fingerpaint. The value of fingerpainting is in the feeling, the touching and the mixing of colours.

> With his own board, Kori has the space and time to study the textures and variations of colour. He started with red and yellow, and now he notices what has happened to his vermilion, having added dollops of white.

Music deepens the fingerpaint dance.
Because fingerpainting is about movement, music enhances this experience. Choose your music carefully - smooth and flowing or light and delicate if you are fingerpainting inside - otherwise there will be fingerpaint everywhere.

Collage

In the part one of this book we looked at how rich and real experiences offer the most for growing minds. Remember how the data soaks in through the senses, and the more experiences we have, the more connections we make in our brain? That is what a well set up natural collage area offers both the children and the adults.

We can tune in and make connections with the nature that we are a part of. We experience this interconnectedness when we are outside looking for and gathering our treasures, and when we enjoy and create with nature's 'ordinary-everyday miracles'. This connectedness grows our sense of belonging at the very deepest level of our being.

Going on **collectors' walks for nature's treasures** offers the chance to soak in nature's rhythms and patterns. The treasures collected will be rich in colours, shapes, textures, subtleties, stories, wonderings and not least, in essence or life force. Children respond to the **essence** of natural treasures at an intuitive level. They collect stones, pebbles, feathers and shells and store them under beds, on window sills or in wardrobes.

Collage basics

While we usually consider collage an inside activity, **the best 'collage' is created outside on Mother Earth.** For millennia children have decorated the sand, the soil, the mud and the rocks. They place their stones, seeds, sticks, flowers, shells and leaves, making patterns on the Earth.

- **When collage is an inside activity, the treasures have to be sorted**
  Children love to gather and sort their treasures. All the acorns in one container, all the acorn cups in another. White icecream containers or flax baskets are suitable for the collage table.
- **Children need a good selection**
  A wide selection offers more patterns to soak in, more subtleties of colour to notice and appreciate, and a greater variety of shapes to make patterns with.
- **Collage working skills**
  Children need to practise and learn the skills of glueing, sticking, taping, tearing, cutting, stapling and using the punch. Once learnt, they use these skills with ease as they create.
- **The space needs to be big enough** for all of the tools they need, and for a decent range of materials to choose from.
- **You'll need shelving alongside the work area** at the children's level to hold the volume of material needed for a successful programme. The big expense will be the table and the shelves. After that, the collage area can be maintained at very little expense. It is, however, an area which needs a lot of love, care and attention to keep it working well for our children
- **Children need bases for their collage:**
  several sizes of cardboard - never paper
  several shapes of card, including circles
  pieces of bark or wood
  large shells or flat stones
- **Children need glue which sticks**. PVA takes a long time to dry but that is something you can teach the children. It doesn't take long to learn that collages and paintings need drying time.

Drawing

Drawing is one of the easiest creative art areas for parents to provide at home; most children will find the ballpoint pen and draw. Because it is the area where children get plenty of practice, if your centre is short of space, provide the play areas we have already described first.

Some materials suitable for the drawing table:
- ballpoint pens
- water-based felt pens and spirit-based felt pens
- pencils and crayons
- pastels and oil pastels
- chalks
- charcoal.

Most importantly, supply paper and card, in a range of colours and in several sizes. Young children enjoy working in miniature, and if we supply suitable smaller pieces of paper and card we facilitate this opportunity.

In general, the finer line the artist is using, the smaller the piece of paper required. Facing a huge piece of paper with a pen can be a bit daunting.

Love, care and attention

In the beginning
In a well-run programme, clay, playdough, paint, fingerpaint and collage will be set up all of the time. Their availability means that children can develop in areas, and at times, that are purposeful to them, and not just when it is convenient for us.

These creative play areas are set up with the same level of care that we would take if we were setting up for a dinner party. This level of care is respect in action; it honours the children in the way we would honour guests.

In the middle
The play areas need to be kept orderly and inviting throughout the session. As soon as a child leaves a play area, their space is tidied and made ready for the next child. It is this prepared space which issues the visual invitation to the newcomer; it says *"There is a place here for you."* This attention to workspace detail keeps the standard of creative play high throughout the length of the session. It ensures that all the media are available for every child and not just for the children who happen to get there first.

In the end
Care taken when cleaning painting equipment, fingerpaint boards, and in the proper storage of the clay makes the next session a breeze to set up.

The bigger picture

Taking care with the creative play areas is part of a bigger picture. When the same care is shown in the whole of the centre, the environment itself communicates to the people in it. It has a certain feel about it which greatly influences how the big people and little people in that space behave. It is very rare to find an environment set up specifically for children which is aesthetically pleasing and which is conducive to concentration. For the concentration required to explore and create, to relate and to learn, centres need to be calm places. Busy, yes - and calm. The centres that achieve this have these eight things in common.

A magic place checklist

❒ You walk in and straight away you feel the calmness.
❒ The music being played is *always* peaceful and relaxing.
❒ The overall colour scheme is low key, peaceful and relaxing. It is based on pastel or natural colours.
❒ The accent colour comes from the equipment, the children's art work, collections of treasures, fresh flowers, and never from the furniture.
❒ There is a lot of natural wood and there are lush plants.
❒ The walls and shelves are uncluttered.
❒ The displays are current.
❒ The whole place is orderly, tidy and clean. Even when the play materials are out being used, orderliness prevails.

If your centre doesn't match up with these eight points, discuss them with your colleagues and find a place where you might begin to make changes. Even very simple changes can eliminate a lot of extraneous stimuli and environmental stress, making the experience much more pleasant for our children and ourselves.

Changes for the better
Just changing your music will work wonders. Music plays a huge role in setting the mood and state of mind for the listeners. Use children's music tapes for singing and music-making sessions, but not for setting the background mood. Similarly, there is no place for commercial radio in a child-friendly centre because the mood it creates is far from calm and peaceful.

Likewise, there is also no place for advertising graphics in child friendly spaces. Our children deserve clear spaces where they are not treated as potential 'buying-units' to be programmed subliminally with vendors' messages. Reserve the display spaces for works of art and treasures which will feed the spirits and souls of all who play and work in your centre.

As all interior designers know, the energy of colours strongly affects human moods and behaviour. Toning down the colour scheme of walls and furniture is a simple way to make the space feel calmer. Shedding any mess and clutter is another simple way to amplify feelings of peace and calmness in a centre.

What now?
It may be as you read through these pages that you have learned new ways to support children's creative art work; ways that are different from what you have done to date.

Be gentle in your choice of response about your past actions in light of new information. Feeling guilty over your past practice is neither loving nor gentle. All of us do the best we can with the knowledge and skills we have at the time. When we know better, we do better. When we learn about better ways, then we can make a choice and do things differently.

What then?
And what happens for new parents at your centre? Will they be left to 'do their thing', doing what they know, only to learn some months later that we do not make or draw for our children? Every adult who makes or draws for a child does it as a **gift** to the child. They certainly do not intentionally set out to deprive children of the opportunities to grow their creativity. When they know better, they too will use their new skills.

Our job in centres is to make sure that new adults know how to work alongside children so that creativity is enhanced. We need to cover the philosophy as part of the introduction to the centre, so that adults know right from the start what is expected of them.

Magic Places

This Earth is truly a magic place. Our children are at home on it, and they can only learn to love it when they get to play outside. Outside they learn to understand and love the nature of which they are a part, getting to know the 'ordinary-miracles': the sky, shells, snails, trees, gold fish, birds, and dandelions. It is we who take young children out to **grow** this sense of wonder and belonging.

Creativity is one of the highest qualities of the human spirit; it is a divine part of our nature. As the guardians of our children, it is we who provide the art materials they need, and we who prepare the environment where they can play at being the Creators they are. Being alongside children as they create is a privilege:

We visit Magic Places together

References

Page 7
- Jensen, Eric, **Brain-Based Learning and Teaching**, Turning Point Publishing, USA 1995

- Pearce, Joseph Chilton, **The Biology of Transcendence: a blueprint for the human spirit,** Park St Press, USA 2002

This book is one of my favourites. It paints on a *huge* canvas: across culture, biology, human development and the human spirit. It is centred around the heart, and the importance of nurturing to transcend societal violence.

- Gerber, Magda, **Dear Parent: caring for infants with respect**, Resources for Infant Educarers (R.I.E. ™), USA 1998

The quality of the relationship starts at birth and Magda offers practical guidelines to build great partnerships with our babies from birth.

Pages 10, 11 & 12
- Herberholz, Donald, and Linderman, Earl, **Developing Artistic and Perceptual Awareness,** Wm. C. Brown, USA 1964

The ideas for these lists around flower experience came directly from their thought-provoking questionnaires.

Page 15
- Hannaford, Carla, **Awakening the Child Heart: handbook for global parenting**, Jamila Nur Publishing, Hawaii, USA 2002

Carla's book is also a favourite of mine. She awakens us to our vital role as adults with children. As Joseph Pearce does, she stresses the value of play for *all* humans, but especially for our children.

Page 34
- Edwards, Betty, **Drawing on the Right Side of the Brain**, Collins, UK 1984

When children reach ten or eleven, because of a shift in the way that their brains work, they want to work in the realism stage. For about ten percent of our children this is easy; for the rest, it isn't. Betty Edwards has done us the greatest service by presenting the skills needed to draw what you see with ease. I recommend you work through her book, either by yourself first, or with your ten-year-old child. Once the skills are learned, you and your child wil be able to draw whatever you wish to depict, realistically.

More great reading

- Hermsen-van Wanrooy, Marianne, **Babymoves**, Baby Moves Publication, Nelson, New Zealand 2002

The unfolding of children's creativity is but one facet in their total development. If your child is still a baby, you have the chance to build a respectful partnership by observing and supporting the unfolding of your child's natural movement. It is during those first months that babies lay down the big beliefs about themselves and the world, beliefs that influence all of their lives, including their yet-to-be-developed creativity. As Magda Gerber says, how must it affect young infants when what they **can** do is not appreciated, and what they cannot do is expected?

- Lorie, Peter, **Wonderchild: rediscovering the magical world of innocence and joy within ourselves and our children**, Simon and Schuster Inc, USA 1989

This book looks at the parent-child partnership from the moment parents decide to have a child through to the time when the child leaves home.

- Armstrong, Thomas, **Awakening Your Child's Natural Genius,** Tarcher Putnam, USA 1991

Thomas Armstrong offers wisdom about all the areas of interest to children, not only creativity. It is a wonderful handbook of ideas for parents of young children.

- Cornell, Joseph, **Sharing Nature with Children**, Dawn Publications, Nevada, California, 1979

- Cornell, Joseph, **Sharing the Joy of Nature with Children**, Dawn Publications, Nevada, California, 1989

These last two books offer great ideas to get the most out of being outside with our children. Each book is full of activities, ranging from the playful to the still and observant. You, the adult, do not need to know the name of any of the plants, birds or creatures that you discover. The genius of these books is that if you 'play the game', you will soak in learning at a very deep level.

Photo: Rebecca Duffy

Notes and ideas too good to forget:

> It took me four years to paint like Raphael, but a lifetime to paint like a child.
>
> Pablo Picasso